Gondor Writing Centre Creative Writing Guide

Book 3

Developing Character

Creative Writing Guide

Book 3

Developing Character

© Copyright Elaine Ouston, Australia 2021

Published by

Morris Publishing Australia

http://morrispublishingaustralia.com

ISBN: 978-0-6452388-1-5

All rights reserved. No part of this publication may be reproduced, stored in a retrieval system, or transmitted, in any form or by means, electronic, mechanical, photocopying, recording or otherwise, without the prior written permission of the copyright holder.

CONTENTS:

Chapter One – Memorable Characters	1
Chapter Two – Following the rules	4
Chapter Three – Personality disorders	14
Chapter Four – Profile of a Killer	25
Chapter Five – Writing Believable Dialogue	32
Character Questionnaire	50

Introduction:

Many people tell me they are going to write a book one day and the idea they have will make it a best seller. Now it is great to have that kind of confidence, but when I ask them what knowledge and experience they have as a writer, they say things like, "I was top of my class in English."

If only it was that simple. There is more to writing a best seller than knowing basic English. Having been through the journey from having ideas to turning them into popular books for children, I can tell you it is not that easy.

To me, saying you can write a best-seller without learning about **the craft of story creation** is like saying you are going to do brain surgery without going to medical school.

50% of writing a great work of fiction is imagination and 50% is technical skill on how to build a great story, but these skills can be learned.

Like all professions, to be the best at what you do, you have to work at it. Many people can tell a story, but if it doesn't excite and intrigue the readers on the first page they won't read on.

These skills are needed whatever you are writing: short story, picture book, chapter books for children, poems, memoirs, novels, etc.

This book and the ones that follow will help you learn those skills.

Chapter One

Memorable Characters

Characters are one of the most important elements in a good story. I like this quote from Ernest Hemingway: When writing a novel, a writer should create living people; people, not characters. A character is a caricature.

Think about the last book you read that stayed in your mind for days. What did you remember the most? Was it the setting, the story, or the main characters? For me it is always the characters. And they are just as important in a short story or poem as they are in a novel. In this guide, we will work on how to make your characters unique and memorable. Now let's look at a few memorable characters we have loved in books.

Tell me the ones that stood out for you. What was it that made them memorable?

The most memorable character in a book I have read recently was Lisbeth, one of the main characters in Stieg Larsson's trilogy that began with *The Girl with the Dragon Tattoo*. Lisbeth had a strong personality disorder, and this disorder, like many, was directly related to her childhood and environment. But this made her very interesting, even though her behaviour was seemingly inconsistent at first.

As I got into the story, I learnt about her background and started to understand her a little more, and my expectations of her actions in any given situation were not far wrong. Even though she broke many of the social rules we live by, and some laws, I developed a liking for her and cared what happened to her.

Later, when we examine personality types, I will include a passage from the second book in the trilogy that tells us what happened to her to make her that way.

These people also stand out:

Plum in Sonya Hartnett's novel *Butterfly*.

Plum is an insecure early teen who feels left out at home, school and in her social life. She has a paranoid/dependent personality. She hates everything about herself and is constantly seeking approval from others. I have included a couple of passages from this novel in previous guides.

The characters in *Big Bang Theory* are all nerds, but what I love about that show is that each one of them has a different personality quirk that makes their inter-personal relationships interesting and humorous. Sheldon clearly sufferers from *Asperger syndrome.*

Doc Martin is Autistic or has Asperger syndrome. This is something people are born with. It is a neurodevelopmental disorder characterized by impaired social interaction, verbal and non-verbal communication, and restricted and repetitive behaviour.

The Good Doctor is also Autistic.

Cleaver Green is a brilliant but self-destructive criminal defence barrister from the TV series Rake. He is described by a critic as a bed-hopping, booze-guzzling, balloon-tripping barrister. He's a dishevelled shambles of a man, with the temper tantrums and gift for self-indulgence of a child. His chief saving graces are a sharp mind, a sharper tongue, and a well-honed ability to launch the charm offensive – whenever he's not simply being offensive.

Now I'm not saying all characters have to be as over the top as these characters, but they have to be different from 'the norm' and memorable.

So, let's look at how to make our characters just as memorable.

For some people, a story starts with a character who pops into their head, demanding their story be told. It develops from there. For others, they start with an idea for a story and then create the characters they need.

However you begin your story, developing your characters so well that you know them as well as you know yourself is vital. Not only does it make it easy to write, but it also makes it much more interesting for your reader. A well-developed character jumps off the page and into the heart and/or mind of your reader and makes them want to stay with the story until the end.

But good characters don't just happen; they are a deliberate blend of many elements arranged to produce a specific result in your particular story. They must fit the role you give them.

For instance, you wouldn't take a character who is covered in tattoos, swears with every second word and make him an English teacher in a girls' private school. It just wouldn't be believable. *Unless* there has been a problem (a cyclone, mass murder of teachers, etc.) and he is all they can get, of course. So, the character needs to fit the role to a certain extent.

How they live and where they live is important to the reader's perception of them. If they live in a wooden shack on the edge of town, we would assume they are poor. And if they live in the most expensive house, we would assume they are rich. Now in a story with a twist, this is not always true, but we want our reader to believe what we show them until we are ready to reveal the truth. So they must act like they belong.

What do you need to make this happen? Today we will be talking at great length about ways to achieve that.

Chapter Two

Following the rules

Here are the rules that you need to follow: We will be going through each in depth.

1. **CREATE REAL PEOPLE NOT CHARACTERS.**

2. **KNOW YOUR CHARACTER AS WELL AS YOU KNOW YOURSELF** – But don't use just your experiences, morals, and values.

3. **STUDY THE PEOPLE AROUND YOU** – Look for their quirks of behaviour, speech patterns, and mannerisms.

4. **MAKE EACH CHARACTER UNIQUE** – Make sure each of your characters is different from the other. We will be studying personality types to make sure we know how to do this.

5. **MAKE THEIR ACTIONS AND SPEECH BELIEVABLE AND CONSISTENT.**

6. **MAKE EACH OF YOUR CHARACTERS ACT DIFFERENTLY IN ANY GIVEN SITUATION** – This is true in real life and should be in your story. It is not enough for you to be able to develop different personalities; you have to ensure you know how they would react in all situations. We will write scenes from the viewpoint of people with different personalities.

7. **STEP INTO THE CHARACTERS HEAD AND *'BE'* THEM WHILE YOU WRITE** – You need to detach yourself from your own personality and become the character.

Later, we will go through a list of personality types, look at how they act and what kind of background might have contributed to that behaviour, and do some exercises.

As part of our examination of personalities, we'll be looking at the profile of people who commit violent crimes and what motivates them to commit these acts. This will be helpful to those of you who are contemplating a crime story. But even if you're not writing crime, we can all learn something valuable by looking at how a profiler works out personality types from their actions. This will help us develop our characters.

Before we start creating characters, we need to have a story to fit them. It is no good creating a bunch of characters and then finding they don't fit our story. Before you create your characters, plot out your story so you know what they have to do. Then create characters with the personalities and skills, etc. needed to play the role.

CREATING YOUR UNIQUE CHARACTERS – Now we get to the fun part – learning how to create the characters to fit our story.

If you have a story idea, keep that story and character in mind as we go through the personality types. You may just find that something we talk about will fit your character and story.

Let's get started by looking in more depth at the rules we talked about:

KNOW YOUR CHARACTER AS WELL AS YOU KNOW YOURSELF:

When creating a character, we tend to use our own experiences, our understanding, values, and characteristics, but that is not enough. Do we really want our characters to be just like us?

Of course we don't, especially if we are writing more than one story. There is nothing worse than reading a second novel from an author and realising that the character in the second one is just a clone of the one in the first with a different name – or finding that all the characters in a novel are the same kind of people, good or bad.

Each character you develop must be different or there is no interpersonal conflict, and the story is boring.

In my fantasy series, *The Mystery of Nida Valley*, the best friend of the main character is the complete opposite of her. Our hero is brave and fearless and doesn't think anything of breaking rules if she feels she has a good reason. Her best friend is a stickler for the rules and a little timid. This creates conflict between them that adds to the entertainment and reality of the story. But as all characters should, they grow and learn from each other as the story progresses.

STEP INTO THE CHARACTERS HEAD AND '*BE*' THEM:

How far you can go to make a character different is answered in part by your own personal experiences and understanding. If you have a difficult time understanding other people's motives, then it will be more difficult for you to explore characters that feel or think differently than you do.

Let's explore that:

Think about these questions. *If you are in a monogamous relationship, would you have an affair for any reason? Why? Why not?* If infidelity is a concept you cannot imagine for yourself, can you empathize with your cheating character well enough to portray him/her accurately and sympathetically?

Conversely, if you find having an affair to be second nature, can you write a faithful character without slipping into an uptight, narrow-minded stereotype?

This is only one scenario. The possibilities are endless for conflict between your own beliefs and your character's.

Could you commit a crime? If you are going to write crime novels, you have to think like a criminal. And you need to think like a law official. Can you objectively do both?

So just in those two genres, romance and crime, you may find it difficult to portray your character's motivation for their acts in a way that makes your reader understand and empathise. In all genres, there is a need for developing strong characters that are both good and evil. Can you do this without allowing your values to come through?

All genres depend on a well-told story with characters that make sense to the reader. All good novels rely heavily on exploring the characters' inner thoughts and motivations. Internal conflicts are more important than external conflicts in many. It is crucial to understand how and why your character is going to act or react in a given situation.

If you have difficulty in understanding other people's actions and the motivation behind them, your characters will all be the same. They will have your morals and beliefs. Like an actor, to make a character real and believable, you need to put yourself in their shoes and 'be' them for the length of the novel. Can you do that?

If you have strong beliefs and values, it may prove too difficult for you to be objective and not come across as judgemental.

How do you overcome this problem? By examining personality types and learning what made them that way.

STUDY PEOPLE AROUND YOU:

One of the best ways to make your characters believable and unique is to look closely at the people you know. Everyone has some kind of personality quirk that makes them distinctive.

It could be an irrational fear of heights, closed spaces, open spaces, crowds, spiders, snakes, etc. And their level of reaction could be anything from total terror to a feeling of mild discomfort.

Some people are so terrified of certain things that their fear becomes a phobia.

Phobias are an important part of how a person behaves. Imagine a character with arachnophobia reacting to the presence of a huge spider in the room. They would most likely scream and run from the room and be unable to continue a conversation until the thing is removed.

A character's deep-seated fears have the ability to expose a little of his or her history and emotional make-up. Introducing those fears into the plotline is also an excellent tool for creating further tension in your story.

Many people have feelings of inadequacy in certain situations or areas of their life, or confidence that is not justified.

They may find it difficult to make friends, or they may have been so badly hurt by someone they loved that they will never love or trust again, or many other things.

Observe the people around you and use their quirks or a combination of them to enhance your character.

I have a fear of closed spaces. I'm Claustrophobic, but I'm getting better at handling it. I once had a fear of deep water and couldn't go out in a boat. I beat that one. And I had a fear of heights ... not quite over that one. Where did these fears come from? The last two from an overprotective mother, but the first one from getting stuck under a house a meter off the ground while trying to save a pet who was stuck in there. It was dark and cold, and it took ages for someone to hear me and come to my rescue.

Think about your fears or phobias or those of people you know.

We are going to talk in great detail about personality types and how to portray them shortly.

Have you ever listened to the speech patterns of those around you? Some people end a sentence with a word that is almost like a question, or with an actual question. Words like 'eh, you know, but, and many more.

Think about ones that you have observed and try writing a paragraph from their perspective.

To help distinguish one character from another, give them a distinctive speech habit, accent, or pattern. All of these things make your character human and believable. But don't go overboard and make it annoying.

MAKE THEIR ACTIONS AND SPEECH BELIEVABLE AND CONSISTENT:

Many stories I receive to edit have an interesting character, and as a reader, I think I understand who they are, but halfway through the story, the writer has them acting in a way that is totally out of character or speaking in a manner that is different.

When this happens in a story, it confuses the reader, makes them care less about the main protagonist and they lose interest in what happens to them.

If you know your characters well, you will know how they will react in *any* given situation, and this will help you make their actions and thoughts consistent through the story.

In saying that, there are reasons that would make someone act out of character. For instance, most meek timid parents would stand up to the most dangerous situation to save their child. This is acceptable deviation from normal behaviour, but in many cases, the writer has a protagonist acting out of character for no apparent reason. However, this could work if they had a strong personality disorder. It could also work if the story was of the growth of a character. But in this last case, the change would be gradual and accompanied by much inner-thought.

So, don't forget to give your characters a human element. Don't try to make them too perfect. Make them different from you.

WE ARE ALL A PRODUCT OF OUR UP-BRINGING:

So including their background in your character profile interview is important. We are all who we are because of the way we were shaped from birth. Our values, manners, morals, speech pattern, accent, and our level of confidence etc, were all instilled in us from birth. Unless we have recognised problems in these beliefs and worked on change, we are still who we were shaped to be.

Now we are never going to put this background information in the story. Though some people do. They write pages of background information that is not relevant to the story. The reason we need to know this information is so we will understand how and why they act the way they do. Any of it that is relevant, and we want the reader to know, we can slot in where needed.

In my short story, *An Unexpected Windfall*, I needed my readers to understand why my main character, who is at first submissive and lacking in confidence, acts as she does. A member of the writers' group that read it called her a wimp and at first she was. In this scene at the beginning, I wanted to show her personality and the reason for it.

'I grimaced at my face in the mirror. A pimple had appeared overnight. I hastily covered it with make-up. My dad's comment at such times during my teen years echoed in my mind. 'You don't plan to go out in public with that ugly blemish, do you? It makes you look hideous'. I didn't miss his teasing comments, or my brother's taunts of puss-face.'

I included that to show that she was teased a lot during her childhood and that is what contributed to her lack of confidence and lack of ability to stand up for herself. By putting it in inner-dialogue, I was also able to show emotion.

Now, I want you to do a couple of simple writing exercises.

I want you to imagine this scene: It is late at night, and you are sitting dozing in front of the TV. Suddenly there is a loud knocking on the window. You rush over and there is a man out in the yard. He is shouting to you to come outside, *now*. When you hesitate, he picks up a brick and heads towards the window with the obvious intention of smashing it.

I want you to write a paragraph or two of the scene from that point, saying what you would be feeling and what you would do?

What would I do? I would open the window and ask him to explain. I wouldn't feel threatened until I had good reason to feel that way, but I would be cautious. I would of course, always have a security screen between him and me. Why would I open the window? Because I'm a trusting soul and I would believe he means well until it was proven otherwise.

There could be many good reasons that he is taking that action; *a fire next door, a tree about to fall, etc.*

But if you were a person who is fearful, you would act in a different way. You might back away and call for help.

In previous workshops, with many people in the room, there were quite a few different reactions to this scenario.

Look at what you have written. If you were writing this scene in a story and the character had a different personality to you, could you convincingly portray what they were feeling. A good writer has to be able to do that.

Let's do one more:

Now imagine this scene: You are standing on a railway platform on your way home from a well-paying job. There is only you and a woman in front of you. She is dressed in very expensive clothes and dripping in jewels. You attempt a conversation, but she dismisses you as if you are not worth the effort. As the train pulls into the station, she pulls a ticket out of her bag and a roll of money drops to the ground. She doesn't notice and rushes forward to get on the train. You bend and pick up the money and move towards the train. What would you do with the money? Be totally honest here.

Write down what you would do and how you would feel about it.

If you said you would hand it in, let's imagine that scene again, but with one difference. You have just been sacked from your job, at home you have five kids and a dependant spouse who needs a critical operation that you now can't afford.

Now what would you do with the money and how would you feel about it?

Once again, if you were writing this scene in a story and it was important that the character acted differently to the way you would, could you convincingly portray what they were feeling and justify their actions so that the reader felt that the scene was believable.

A good writer has to be able to do that.

So, when you write a character profile, remember that a person's background and present circumstances will make them act in different ways to what you would. And sometimes, as we explored before, in different ways to what they normally would.

We will be exploring this in more depth shortly.

MAKE EACH OF YOUR CHARACTERS ACT DIFFERENTLY IN ANY GIVEN SITUATION:

This is true in real life and should be in your story. It is not enough for you to be able to develop different personalities; you have to ensure you know how they would react in all situations.

Why? Because the characters in your story will have different roles to play. After we go through the personality types, we will look at a scene where this is especially important.

Now I want to go through a list of the recognised personality disorders. Why? Because many of us suffer from mild cases of these disorders (typically called behavioural traits) and if you give your characters even one of these traits, they will be believable. I think you will recognise many of them and be able to relate them to either yourself or others. I know I can. Some of us have very mild forms of these disorders, others have very strong forms. It is interesting to note that it is recognised that many of them are caused by childhood experiences or by our up-bringing.

Understanding and knowing these disorders will help you create interesting characters.

Chapter Three

Personality Disorders

To be a writer you also have to be an amateur psychologist. There is no 'normal' personality. Every one of us is different.

Those with serious psychological personality disorders have traits that cause them to feel and behave in socially distressing ways, typically resulting in discord and instability in many aspects of their lives. Depending on the specific disorder, these personalities are generally described in negative terms such as hostile, detached, needy, antisocial, or obsessive.

But many of us have mild forms of these disorders. That is what makes us unique. It is not a problem.

While many other psychological disorders fluctuate in terms of symptom presence and intensity, personality disorders typically remain relatively constant throughout life.

As I said before, many of us have these traits, but to a lesser extent than those diagnosed with disorders. As we go through the list, I'm sure you will recognise these traits in many people you know who are perceived to be 'normal' – whatever normal may be.

Let's look at some of these character traits. These are just some of the milder forms of behaviour that are familiar:

Hyper-anxiety: Always fearful of something happening to them or their loved ones.

Controlling – manipulative: Need to be in charge. Believes that no one can do things better than they can.

A perfectionist: Nothing is ever right. They have to do tasks over and over again and are never happy with the result. They also insist people close to them do the same and will redo many things they think isn't done well enough.

Antisocial Personality: APD is characterized by lack of empathy or conscience, a difficulty controlling impulses and by manipulative behaviour. This is often found in criminals, vandals, and people who are cruel to animals or defenceless people.

Paranoid: Believes that everyone is out to get them. Live their life in fear. They believe no-one likes them and the world is out to get them. Most also believe that everything that happens to them is someone else's fault.

I want you to write 5 scenes showing how you think a person with a mild form of each of these disorders would act in this situation in the paragraph that follows: Write them from the perspective of the person you bumped into.

You are walking through a mall, and you accidentally bump into someone who is carrying a bag of groceries. They spill over the floor. The person turns to you and ...

Keep it simple and brief.

***

Asperger's syndrome is also a fairly common disorder that we meet in our life and one that makes interesting characters.

This syndrome, also known as Asperger disorder or autism, is one of a group of neurodevelopmental disorders that have effects on an individual's behaviour, use of language and communication, and pattern of social interactions.

It was formerly characterized as one distinct autism spectrum disorder, although this syndrome was considered to be at the milder, or higher-functioning, range of this spectrum.

People with Asperger's syndrome have normal to above-average intelligence but typically have difficulties with social interactions and often have pervasive, absorbing interests in special topics.

The negative characteristics include: Lack of social awareness; lack of interest in socializing/making friends; difficulty making and sustaining friendships; inability to infer the thoughts, feelings, or emotions of others; either gazing too intently or avoiding eye contact; lack of changing facial expression, or use of exaggerated facial expressions; lack of use or comprehension of gestures; inability to perceive nonverbal cues or communications; failure to respect interpersonal boundaries.

They are unusually sensitive to noises, touch, odours, tastes, or visual stimuli; inflexibility and over-adherence to or dependence on routines; and stereotypical and repetitive motor patterns such as hand flapping or arm waving.

Positive characteristics of people with Asperger syndrome have been described as beneficial in many professions and include: the increased ability to focus on details, the capacity to persevere in specific interests without being swayed by others' opinions, the ability to work independently, the recognition of patterns that may be missed by others, intensity, and an original way of thinking.

As I mentioned before, this is the personality of Doc Martin, in the show on TV, and Sheldon in The Big Bang Theory. What kind of role do you think they would suit?

Write a paragraph using a character with this personality.

Now let's look at the more serious disorders. Many people have a mild form of these personality traits or disorders.

Classification of Personality Disorders: According to the Diagnostic and Statistical Manual (DSM-IV-TR), there are ten different personality disorders categorized into three main groupings or clusters. Some are caused by chemical imbalance in the brain some by experiences in life.

Cluster A: Odd or Eccentric Behaviours

Schizoid Personality

Individuals with schizoid personality are characteristically detached from social relationships and show a restricted range of expressed emotions. Those with SPD may be perceived by others as sombre and aloof and often are referred to as 'loners'.

Schizoid personality disorder isn't as disabling as schizophrenia and, unlike schizophrenia, does not result in a disconnection from reality. Most experts agree that schizoid personality disorder, like many mental health disorders, is caused by a combination of genetics and social environment during early development. This description can also fit a person who is autistic or has Asperger.

They would be the kids in the playground, sitting in a corner with a book, ignoring all around them. Or the adult who lives alone and rarely ventures out of their house except to shop. They avoid looking anyone in the eye and shuffle if you corner them to ask how they are. This is primarily caused by experiences in childhood.

Psychoactive drugs are also linked to the development of this disorder and stressful events such as death of a loved one, or divorce can trigger the symptoms.

Write a paragraph using a character with this personality.

***

Paranoid Personality

Those with a serious form of this personality are typically distrustful and suspicious of others. Although they are prone to unjustified angry or aggressive outbursts when they perceive others as disloyal or deceitful, those with PPD more often come across as emotionally "cold" or excessively serious. They believe no-one likes them and the world is out to get them. Once again, psychologist believe this disorder is caused by experiences in childhood.

They are usually people who were picked on, berated, and told how worthless they were.

Write a paragraph using a character with this personality.

***

Schizotypal Personality

This personality is characterized both by a need for isolation, as well as odd, outlandish, or paranoid beliefs. In social situations, they may show inappropriate reaction or not react at all, or they may talk to themselves. This can be caused by an imbalance of brain chemicals or by a reaction to trauma in childhood.

This is the disorder that I believe Lisbeth from *The Girl with The Dragon Tattoo* suffered from. What caused hers? This prologue in the sequel, *The Girl Who Played with Fire*, tells us. She was thirteen at the time.

'She lay on her back fastened by leather straps to a narrow bed with a steel frame. The harness was tight across her rib cage. Her hands were manacled to the sides of the bed.

'She had long since given up trying to free herself. She was awake, but her eyes were closed. If she opened her eyes, she would find herself in darkness; the only light a strip that seeped in above the door. She had a bad taste in her mouth and longed to be able to brush her teeth. She was listening for the sound of footsteps, which would mean he was coming. She had no idea how late at night it was, but she sensed that it was too late for him to visit her.

'She marked off another day in her bed. It was the forty-third day of her imprisonment.'

Write a paragraph using a character with this personality.

***

Cluster B: **Dramatic, Emotional, or Erratic Behaviour**

Antisocial Personality.

APD is characterized by lack of empathy or conscience, a difficulty controlling impulses and manipulative behaviours. This disorder is sometimes also referred to as psychopathy or sociopathy, however, Antisocial Personality Disorder is the clinical terminology used for diagnosis. Once again, this disorder can be caused by an imbalance of brain chemicals or by a reaction to trauma in childhood.

Many criminals have this disorder. So, if you are writing crime, study it in detail.

Write a paragraph using a character with this personality.

***

Borderline Personality

This condition is caused by an imbalance of brain chemicals that interfere with an individual's ability to regulate emotion. The characteristic emotional instability results in dramatic and abrupt shifts in mood, impulsivity, poor self-image and tumultuous interpersonal relationships.

Borderlines are highly sensitive to rejection, and fear of abandonment may result in frantic efforts to avoid being left alone, such a suicide threats and attempts.

Write a paragraph using a character with this personality.

***

Narcissistic Personality

NPD is characterized primarily by grandiosity, need for admiration, and lack of empathy. Narcissism occurs in a spectrum of severity, but the pathologically narcissistic tend to be extremely self-absorbed, intolerant of others' perspectives, insensitive to others' needs and indifferent to the effect of their own egocentric behaviour.

It is believed to be caused by: Parenting style either excessive pampering or criticism, genetic changes, or changes in the structure or functioning of brain.

Risk factors may include: Family history of mental health disorders, unpleasant family life during childhood or conduct disorder during childhood.

This is, I believe, the personality of Donald Trump. Many psychologists agree with me.

Write a paragraph using a character with this personality.

***

Histrionic Personality

Individuals with this personality exhibit a pervasive pattern of excessive emotionality and attempt to get attention in unusual ways, such as bizarre appearance or speech.

With rapidly shifting, shallow emotions, histrionics can be extremely theatrical, and constantly need to be the centre of attention.

Women with this trait are commonly referred to as "Drama Queens".

The exact cause of this condition is unknown but major factors include; mental health, which makes one unable to love, traumatic experiences; such as death of a close loved one or divorce of the parents.

There can be inherited factors – the disorder that runs in the family or environmental factors like lack of criticism or punishment as a child. The more severe walk the streets muttering to themselves.

I think we all know someone like this.

Write a paragraph using a character with this personality.

***

Cluster C: Anxious, Fearful Behaviour

Avoidant Personality

Those with avoidant personalities are often hypersensitive to rejection and unwilling to take social risks. People with this personality display a high level of social discomfort, timidity, fear of criticism, and feelings of inadequacy and inferiority. They avoid activities that involve interpersonal contact.

Causes: Family history of avoidant personality traits or disorder, neurotransmitter dysfunction or authoritarian parenting.

Write a paragraph using a character with this personality.

***

Dependent Personality

People with dependent personality typically exhibit a pattern of needy and submissive behaviour and rely on others to make decisions for them.

Dependent personalities require excessive reassurance and advice and are extremely sensitive to criticism or disapproval.

Common causes are: Abusive relationships: People who have a history of abusive relationships have a higher risk of a DPD diagnosis.

Childhood trauma: Children who have experienced child abuse (including verbal abuse) or neglect may develop DPD. It may also affect people who experienced a life-threatening illness during childhood.

Family history: Someone with a family member who has DPD or another anxiety disorder may be more likely to have a DPD diagnosis.

Certain cultural and religious or family behaviours: Some people may develop DPD due to cultural or religious practices that emphasize reliance on authority. But passivity or politeness alone is not a sign of DPD.

Write a paragraph using a character with this personality.

***

Obsessive-Compulsive Personality

Individuals with OCPD are so focused on order and perfection that their lack of flexibility interferes with productivity and efficiency.

They can also be workaholics, preferring the control of working alone, as they are afraid that work completed by others will not be done correctly.

Many people have this trait in some form. And, in many cases it is a good thing. They make great workers where precision is important.

Causes: Several theories suggest that people with OCPD may have been raised by parents who were unavailable and either overly controlling or overly protective. Also, as children they may have been harshly punished. The OCPD traits may have developed as a sort of coping mechanism to avoid punishment, in an effort to be "perfect" and obedient.

Write a paragraph using a character with this personality.

***

How many of you recognised some of these tendencies in either yourselves, or others they know? I know I did.

So, what is normal? Who knows? But you can see that using even a mild form of one of these so-called personality disorders would make your character memorable like Doc Martin, Sheldon, Lisbeth or many others in blockbuster novels and on the screen.

Now we are going to do a writing exercise using the following mild forms of behaviour: Ones you are more likely to want in your stories.

Hero complex: They think they have to fix everything and that they are the only ones you can rely on to do it. They try to take over every task, but not because they are being manipulative, because they care and want to do everything for you. They have a need to care for, help, and rescue people.

<u>Fearlessness</u>: They rush into every situation without thinking of the consequences. They think they are untouchable, and nothing will ever happen to them.

<u>Passive, nervous, lacking confidence:</u> They believe they can't do anything right and so mostly don't try.

Write me a paragraph of the following scene with people with these different personalities in it.

The scene is in a schoolyard. It's lunch time and the kids are sitting under a shelter eating their lunch. 3 teachers are in attendance. Each one has one of the 3 personalities I mentioned. Suddenly, they are alerted to a gunman coming towards them. What would each person do?

Chapter Four

THE PROFILE OF A KILLER

I have been reading the book, *Profiling – the psychology of killers*. I am going to share a couple of the cases from the book to reinforce how destructive some of the personalities we just learnt about can become if they are extreme and left untreated.

This will be helpful to those of you who are contemplating a crime story, but I think we can all learn something valuable by looking at how a profiler works out the personality types of people who committed crimes from their actions. This will help us develop our characters.

So first, let's look at the questions the profilers ask, and what they look for.

If you are writing a crime novel or including a crime in your novel, these are the questions you would ask to set up the profile of the criminal and the plot to make it believable.

1. Did the criminal have a planned routine or fantasy they appeared to be following when they set the crime in motion?

2. Are there factors to explain why the criminal chose that day to find and kill or rob his victim?

3. How did he select his victims, by type or just opportunity, and what does this reveal about his motivation?

They study how the victim's body was disposed of afterwards, whether it was simply left at the scene of the killing, disposed of elsewhere, or dismembered and dumped.

At the crime scene, they look for anyone showing a particular interest in the case or seeking to become involved.

The scene will usually show them if the killer is organized or not. This distinction relates to different personalities and background. Let's examine that.

THE ORGANISED KILLER:

They would leave the body where it could not be easily found or buried carefully with signs of disturbance eliminated as much as possible. They would leave little or no trace of evidence at the scene or on the body.

The characteristics of an organized killer are usually a person having an outwardly normal appearance and behaviour, and adequate social skills that allows them to persuade a victim to trust them to the point where they can be brought under the criminal's influence.

Many hold jobs and are in a committed relationship.

DISORGANIZED OR IMPULSIVE KILLER:

The body would be left where the attack occurred or not well hidden. The attack would be frenzied and the wounds many.

The personality type would be that of someone who has been abused as a child, has no social skills, and so is dismissed by society, and is angry at the world. Sometimes, they pick on a particular type of person. One who resembles the abuser or one who resembles a parent who did not help them. *They are lashing out to show their anger and power.*

THE VICTIM:

Sometimes, the victim is profiled. This information can also relate to the crime and the person responsible.

For example, if the victim followed a set routine, this might suggest that the crime was organized and planned carefully. The perpetrator had studied the victim's routine to know where the target would be at the time of the crime and perhaps frequented the same places.

The victim's type of work might also reflect more light on the crime, since the degree of risk undergone by the victim would be greater in some jobs than others: a prostitute has the highest risk, involving casual contact with strangers on the fringes of society and as someone who might not be missed for some considerable time. Perhaps the most low-risk would be the police and armed services since they are in close contact with their colleagues and peers and would be immediately missed and their disappearance investigated by professionals.

Let's look at some actual cases.

CASE ONE:

The trailside killer: Bodies of young women were found on a walking trail in a park. Several of the victims were found in a kneeling position and most were shot in the back of the head.

The profiler said that probably meant that the killer had sneaked up on them from behind, which suggested that he had low self-esteem, was shy and reclusive, unhappy about his appearance, or possibly suffering a speech impediment or disfiguring of some kind.

His selection of secluded sites suggested he knew the park well and so was local. As his victims were white, they assumed he too was white (but why – it could well have been a racist killing).

His attention to detail suggested a reasonable level of intelligence and so they thought he was probably a blue-collar worker or above.

His later escalation to rape and stabbings suggested a level of aggression. This made them consider that he might have been in prison at some time for aggressive behaviour.

They thought he would be in his 30s and in his younger years may have shown the 3 classic indicators of his lack of self-esteem: bed wetting, cruelty to animals, and a tendency to start fires. He may have committed rape or acts of violence against women before.

He was caught, mostly by mistakes he made; shooting a second victim in a double murder attempt, but not killing him. The victim was able to give a good description. Then, while they were searching for him, he killed someone he had worked with when she went with him to buy a car. She had told her boyfriend where she was going and who with. They went to his house, found her belongings, and arrested him. He subsequently confessed and told them the location of the body.

The profile was accurate. He was a person with a stutter, yellowed teeth, and a bad temper. He had been raised by domineering parents. Their pressure had sapped his confidence, increased his stutter, and made him shy and resentful. He had miss-treated animals and molested his cousins at 17. He had been married and had three kids, but his insatiable sex drive had ended the marriage.

So once again, a product of his up-bringing.

CASE TWO:

A woman rang police and said a man had jumped into her car at a traffic light and driven off with her children. On investigation, the police found her story difficult to believe. *One of the reasons was* because the traffic light she spoke of was set to operate only if there was an approach of a vehicle from the quiet side road.

A camera indicated that there were no such vehicles for two hours either side of the time she claimed the incident took place. Therefore, she would not have had to stop.

They believed she had hurt or killed the children but had found no bodies. A profiler was called in to see if they thought her guilty.

He gave the following profile of a mother who would kill her children.

A troubled young woman probably with limited education, who had grown up in an abusive and unhappy family with real money worries, and who consequently suffered from depression, perhaps with a history of suicide attempts.

In terms of the reason for the crime, rejection by a lover who might otherwise have presented an escape from her limited circumstances might have spurred her to take the life of her two sons so they or she didn't have to suffer her childhood fate.

They were right again. It was revealed that the mother had a background of this kind and when her husband had filed for divorce, she began a relationship with a rich man who would take her in, but not her sons. Fearing being left poor again, she drove her sons into a lake and let them drown. Her fear of poverty was so strong that she took her sons lives to ensure her lover would take care of her. She was found guilty and given 30 years.

These cases prove what we have talked about previously. Both of these people acted the way they did because of their background.

This reinforces the fact that the background of your characters is something you MUST have firmly in your head before you begin the story, because it will influence their behaviour.

As I said previously, before you can develop characters, you have to have an idea for a story and know what it is they are going to have to achieve. There is no point developing a character that will not fit the story you want to tell.

So, our first exercise is to develop an idea or work on the one you already have, using the basic formula in *Creative Writing Guide, Book One, Turning Your Idea into A Story.*

The setting is also important. No point creating an unfit, unconfident man and asking him to climb a mountain to save someone.

THE CHARACTERS:

Now we are going to develop the characters for our story. In the last pages are interview questions to ask your characters. Think about your story and the kind of character that you would need to make the story believable. Remember, they don't have to be 'normal' they can be 'different', but they have to be believable.

Fill in the sheet for your main character. Do the same for your other characters before you write your story.

THE STORY:

Even though you have written a lengthy description of each character, the only way your reader should know about their background is by their thoughts, actions, attitudes, or words. We don't launch into a mass of narrative that says who they are and where they come from, or why they act the way they do, we let the story, setting, and the characters tell the reader that. Sprinkle in the details, so the reader gradually becomes aware of why the character is behaving the way he is.

When you know your character well, you don't have to worry about writing something contradictory to your character's nature. When you can picture your character as a living, breathing, larger than life person, then you can make him/her jump off the page.

The more real a character is to you, the more real they will be to your readers.

The first two pages of a novel should introduce your character, give us an idea of the situation they are in, and a hint of what is to come.

Go to your bookcase and select a bestselling novel. Open it and read the first two pages.

Write down what you learnt about the main character and see if you can do the same for your story.

The other thing that will kill your character is the dialogue he speaks. Let's look at the best way to address that.

Chapter Five

Writing Believable Dialogue

It doesn't matter how well a novel is plotted or how exciting the action is, if the dialogue is flat or forced you lose your reader. Learning to write dialogue is a major challenge.

Nothing can kill a character faster than the words they speak. Dialogue is one of the main ways a reader gets to know a character.

There is good dialogue and there is bad dialogue and, depending on which you are writing, it will make or break your story. Nothing engages a reader more than realistic dialogue and nothing disgruntles a reader more than a phrase that is contrived, clichéd and unnatural; it will pull a reader away from your lovingly crafted prose quicker than a flat character or a thin plot could ever do.

It is not too much of a surprise then, to discover that writing dialogue is one of the most challenging elements of fiction writing and one that takes time to master. Good writing requires curiosity, imagination and inspiration. It also requires a knowledge of mechanics and craft.

Dialogue is particularly tough. Any writer who thinks writing dialogue is easy is probably not writing good dialogue.

The character's personality is revealed in every word they speak, and in their actions, and it's the writer's job to make sure the dialogue is appropriate and sounds natural for that character.

From your character's speech, you should learn at least:

* Their personality

* Their age

* Their education level

* A general idea of where they come from

* Their relationship to the character they are addressing

* Their mood

How can you learn to do this? There are several things you need to do.

Listen to how people talk. This is the best way to learn about speech patterns and natural dialogue. People have many different methods of verbal expression, and they vary depending on who they are talking to, what they are talking about, their mood and their upbringing. Taking notes from real life will greatly improve the authenticity of your dialogue.

One of the best ways is to go to a busy café and sit near someone of the age and personality of your character. Listen to their dialogue and take notes on their style of speaking.

Be careful when writing the speech of small children. Listen to someone in the age group or question them about your topic to see what they know. Many people put words into children's mouths that they wouldn't have learnt or understood the meaning of at the age portrayed.

Let's look at the changes in speech when talking to different age groups and with different relationships between the characters. We'll do a simple exercise.

Imagine this scene: Someone walks into a shop and interrupts a busy, already-serving-a-customer salesperson, and asks her where to find the toothpaste. This how I imagine it.

A shy, hesitant child of about 10: Where's the toothpaste?

Salesperson: 'Aisle 2. Oh, wait a moment. I'm busy right now. I'll show where it is as soon as I finish this.'

A harassed mother with a screaming baby in the pram: 'Where would I find the toothpaste?'

Salesperson: With a look of sympathy, she might say, "Aisle 2, sweetheart."

An impatient man carrying a briefcase: 'Point me to the toothpaste.'

Salesperson: With an impatient stare to match his, she might say, 'I'll be with you in a moment.'

Her teenage daughter: 'Mum, where's the toothpaste?'

Salesperson: 'Can't you see I'm busy, honey. Just wait.'

Try writing the answers as you see it. When writing make sure you vary the speech of your characters depending on who they are talking to.

The other thing you must do is give your character a distinct voice.

Accents and speech patterns differ from state to state, country to country. The education level of your characters, their age, their gender, and personality affect the way they talk. All of your characters need to have a distinct voice.

A reader should be able to read a line of speech and identify which character has spoken. There are many techniques for achieving this.

You may give your character a distinct accent, use habitual phrases or mistakes, which they tend to repeat, or vary the speech patterns through the correct or incorrect use of grammar.

How many of you know someone who repeats a word or phrase at the end of every sentence? Like 'you know', 'eh', 'don't ya think'. 'What ya recon', 'Like, you know'. Speech patterns of mispronounced words like, 'gunna', 'havta' etc are common in the speech of even highly educated Australians. If your character has the background that would make him or her use these words, use them, but be persistent and *don't over-do it.*

Working with dialects:

Be careful if you decide to use a strong dialect or accent. You may want to capture the essence of the dialect to make your character real to the setting, but it's extremely difficult to write hundreds of pages in a foreign accent. It is also hard to read. And you must be very careful to make sure that the misspelt words are easily recognised by your reader. If the reader has to limp through the speech pattern and learn what the character is trying to say, it makes reading too hard and you will lose them. And if you slip up and miss a few, the tone of the book changes in mid-stream and it's jarring for the reader.

The same is true of writing historical fiction. Trying to capture the real sound of Victorian English is hard. And, if all you know of the French language is "Oui, oui," it becomes a farce. In some cases, it may be best to write the dialogue normally, and let the setting be the clue to the character's background and dialect.

Study the language of the era, country, or area by reading a book or watching a movie that depicts it clearly.

If you decide to use misspelt words to recreate a dialect, this mangling of the English language is going to put a computer's spell-check into overdrive. Seeing so many deliberately misspelt words underlined in red may make you miss the ones you should see.

If you put in an unusual spelling or an unusual name, add it to the dictionary straight away to avoid having red underlines on your pages. Then, if you misspell the strange name or the deliberately misspelt word it will underline it for you.

One way to handle dialect is to use just a few words to give flavour to the dialogue. It could be as simple as having the character refer to his grandmother as 'Meema' or 'Grandmere'. When this is used, we know who has spoken.

If you aren't familiar with the dialect or foreign accent of the setting, it's wise not to go crazy trying to recreate it.

Unintentional formality:

Some problems in dialogue come from an unintentional formality that creeps into the writing. Instead of writing, "Hey, what's your problem," a novice may write, "I don't quite understand what the problem is." It sounds stilted and very formal. There are characters who would talk like that but be careful not to make all of your characters speech that formal.

One way to see if the speech sounds natural is to rehearse the conversation before you write it. Choose a time when no one else is around and say aloud the words you are going to write. Or ask a family member or writer friend to do it with you. Go through the scene and read each character's dialogue aloud. If the dialogue is unnatural or formal, chances are it will be evident.

On the other hand, if the dialogue is too informal, it tends to sound unbelievable. No one can say, "Got ya!" or "That right?" or "Ga day Cobber", too many times without it becoming ridiculous.

If this is one of the speech habits of your character use it not more than a couple of times on a page.

At some point, the characters will need to have a substantial conversation to grow and develop. Weak dialogue can be a sign of a weak or undeveloped character.

Don't obsess about grammar in dialogue:

Most people don't use correct grammar when they speak, and you shouldn't when you are writing dialogue. People speak in incomplete sentences, leave out words, and interrupt each other. Relaxing the grammar can only help your dialogue to be more believable. 'Want to come to the beach?' or 'Comin to the beach?' is far more common than, 'Do you want to come to the beach?' 'It's hot, eh!' Or 'Hot, eh!' would be more common than, 'Isn't it hot today?'

Let's look at this phrase and examine how different people would say it.

"I cannot believe that you would do such a thing."

From the point of view of:

A teen: *"Why'd ya do that?"*

A mother: *"What do you think you are doing?"*

A Professor: *"What makes you believe you have the right to do that?"*

A street-tough man or woman: *"What the f**k?"*

Don't Overuse slang, stereotypes and Ummms!

Using local dialect or slang is okay if you decide your character speaks that way, but don't overuse it. If your character speaks only in slang, then it is not believable.

Words like: Youse, bobby dazzler, cool, chick, Shelia, buedy mate, dag, dipstick, arvo, bloody oath, etc should be used sparingly.

Throw in one or two occasionally to keep in character but let his personality and speech pattern tell the reader who he is. Too much of this can distract or alienate your reader. They will also age your work.

In real speech, people take time to think about what they are saying and 'Ummming' and 'Ahhhing' is commonplace. But, to keep the dialogue economical and interesting, use this sparingly. You could use 'Ummmm …' at the start of a sentence if the character is unsure how to answer the question or trying to find a way out of admitting guilt.

Avoid Anachronisms in Dialogue

When a writer is caught up in a zone, it's easy to let the creative process take over. It's wonderful when it happens but read the draft carefully for any unintentional anachronisms that may have crept into the work.

It's highly unlikely that a teen in Victorian England would shout "Holy Crap!" when surprised. Nor would an adult from that period pass a friend on the street and say, "Hey, what's up?" Although these examples are extreme, small anachronisms do show up and need to be revised. Make sure your speech suits the setting and the era.

Write what you think they would say:

What would a teen in Victorian England say when surprised?

What would an adult from that period, greeting a passing a friend on the street, say?

Make sure the speech in your story suits the setting and the era.

Use dialogue to move the story forward:

In addition to being realistic, dialogue must be purposeful. Read your dialogue and ask whether it has a function. Does it establish tone or mood? Does it reveal anything about the plot or characters? Does it add to the relationship that the reader is building with the speaker? Does it add or create conflict? Does it move the story forward? *If it doesn't have a purpose, delete it.*

If your characters are walking down the street to go where the next scene will take place, don't have them making small talk on the way. Cut to the next scene. This lifts the pace of the story.

Avoid scenes in which characters talk a lot without moving the plot forward. Have them get right to it. For example, when we bump into someone on the street or over the back fence or in a bar, we typically go through a lot of, "How you doing?" "Fine." "Been awhile." "Man, it's been hot." "Yeah, we need rain." "How's the family?" "Fine, just fine. Thanks for asking." This is fine for real life, but not in a manuscript. There should be a purpose to this meeting.

It should move the story forward in some way. Get to the point of that purpose.

If a policeman comes to the door of someone he knows to question them about a crime, don't have them chatting about the weather, or having a cup of tea first, get to the point of the visit. "Morning, Mary? I need to talk to you about the body we found in your freezer."

Sometimes the use of misdirection helps to break up the he said/she said tennis match type dialogue. Have characters answer a question with a question of their own. Or have them ignore a question and say something unrelated to it. Have a subtext in which they say one thing but are thinking another, or the larger meaning of their words strikes a chord in your reader because you had used foreshadowing to tell the reader what the main character doesn't know. These techniques create tension and irony.

I love the way small children respond to questions. At a school visit, I had been reading a story to the grade ones and at the end, I asked questions about the animal characters. "What do wombats eat?" I asked. A few children told me, but when I asked a small girl who had her hand up, she held up her arm and said, "I hurt my elbow." This threw me right off track of course, so I had to go and inspect the elbow and sympathize before I could go back to my questions. People do this all the time.

Here is an example:

"Want to come to the shops?" Mary said, as she walked into the room.

Jane looked up and frowned. "What's that you're wearing?"

"It's my new top."

Jane nodded. "Nice. Can you pick me up some milk?"

Have you ever had this kind of thing happen to you?

Break up dialogue with action:

Breaking up the dialogue with action or setting is especially useful when handling large sections of speech that a reader may find tedious.

Including actions alongside dialogue also gives the reader a sense of the conversation taking place in the real world, which elevates the conversation above mere words on a page, but still try not to have a whole page of dialogue.

Adding a little setting information can help create the mood of the exchange. Like in this exchange.

Mary headed to the door. "Just going to see Jane. Back soon."

John stared at the glow of the setting sun that stained the horizon blood-red as he listened to her words. The wind whispered through the trees echoing what was in his mind, 'She's lying again.'

Re-write the following scene, putting setting and action through this exchange to help create mood and break up the text.

Place: Child's bedroom. Characters: Mother and son.

Son: "I'm not getting up. I don't want to go to school today."

Mother: "You have to."

"I don't. School's dumb."

"It's sports day. You like sport."

"Don't. The coach hates me. Never lets me play."

"Well, if you don't get up now, I'll take away the Game Boy for a week."

"What! You can't."

"Oh, yes I can."

"Alright. I'm up."

Speaker attribution:

While it is best to break up the dialogue with action or setting, if you have to use attribution, use "he/she said" for almost exclusively or use their name.

This is the least obtrusive attribution. Avoid things like "demanded," "countered," "insisted," "shouted," etc. They reflect lazy writing because they tell the reader things rather than showing through good word choice.

Instead of writing, "Tell me," she demanded. You could use an exclamation mark and action to show she was angry. Mary slammed her hand on the table. "Tell me!"

The use of "muttered" or "whispered" is okay as it is difficult to show quiet speech with words, but you could say, *Jim could hardly hear her reply,* to show that she spoke softly.

Never use actions, such as, laugh, cough, spewed, as tags. As in: 'I loved it,' she laughed. We do not laugh words, we speak them. The correct way to write this would be. She laughed and said, 'I loved it.' Or with a chuckle, she said, "I loved it."

Delete attributions when you can. This is simple when only two characters populate a scene, more complicated with three or more. But the different speech patterns etc, that we spoke about earlier, should enable the reader to know who is speaking with only an occasional attribution. Three or more speakers in a scene require more attributions and/or more action to clue your readers in without being clunky about it and having enough 'saids' to drive them nuts.

Use a mixture of 'saids' and action like in this example:

"I never said I'd – ," Jack said.

Helen cut in. "Not in so many words."

"You two make me sick!" Carl slammed his drink on the table.

Jack glared at Carl. "Who gives a damn what you think?"

Get rid of almost every 'ly' adverb in your speaker attributions. If a character says something "hysterically," let his or her words and actions show the hysteria.

Mary flung her hands in the air, her face glowed bright red. "Why would you ask me that again! I already told you once!"

Write this scene using action and dialogue: Jack was angry. He walked into the room and told his son he was a lazy slob and should clean his room.

Make the dialogue and actions tell us his mood.

* * *

Use contractions for informal speech:

It is common to use contractions to make speech sound more natural. 'I would not do that', sounds very stilted when it is read. 'I wouldn't do that', is much more natural.

This is also a subtle way of differentiating characters. A character that doesn't use contractions comes across as formal, maybe even stiff, or stuffy, compared with one who does use them.

A good way to help define character is to have someone who speaks formally and some that don't.

Use ellipsis when you want a speaker's voice to trail off. Use a dash when she's interrupted by another character or by an action.

   "I ... didn't mean to ..." Mary bowed her head.

Jack glared at her. "Well, you should watch what you're –"

Mark stepped between them. "Leave her alone, Jack."

Position of tags:

You can place speech tags at the beginning, middle, or end of speech, or use action to break up the dialogue.

"I can't believe our luck,' Jim said, "another lotto win." He grabbed Mary in a bear hug. "I knew it was our turn."

When experienced, a writer instinctively knows the most effective use of tags and when to leave them out completely. Read the passage of dialogue out loud. It if the tags grate take them out or find a way to replace them.

Don't use dialogue to dump information:

This is where trust in your reader is essential. If you have done your job well, the reader will be able to follow the story as it slowly unfolds, without a character speaking for the sole purpose of filling in a back story, reminding the reader of past details or over-explaining. Information dumps are unnatural, lazy and annoying. Don't do it.

Here is an example:

"Mark, could you stay for a while until Mary, my sister with the twins, gets here?" Jane paused for a moment. "That's right, you guys used to hang out together all the time, before Mary moved to Brisbane when she married Tom. I bet you haven't seen her for ages. You'll probably be happy to see her then."

If it is necessary for the information to be there, use dialogue from both, so it doesn't seem such a dump. *Re-write that by using dialogue from both.*

Use dialogue to add to the pace of the story:

As with all elements of writing fiction, you are in control of the pace. In urgent situations, when you want to pick up the pace and increase tension, leave out or limit narration and tags.

'Look out there is a tiger about to pounce on you', would become, 'Tiger! Run!'

To slow the pace and build suspense, use monologues and longer sections of narration.

As she walked off the dais, her mother hugged her. "I knew this day would come. I dreamed about the day you would graduate as a doctor. Congratulations."

Write this scene with two or three of her friends waiting for her instead of her mother. Obviously, the scene will change from a slow pace to a more excited event.

***

Pay attention to always portraying what a character will and will not talk about, their level of intelligence and sense of humour will also create the difference. This is why developing our characters by interviewing them, as we did earlier, was so important.

In the previous chapter, I mentioned personality types we know and recognise. We are going to touch on those again in our next exercise. Everyone has some kind of personality quirk that makes them distinctive. This will influence their speech.

These are personality traits that are common and affect the way people talk and relate to others:

Fears that become phobias

Feelings of inadequacy

Fear of intimacy

Super ego

Let's look again at the personality classifications we are going to use and the behaviour that is attached to them.

Antisocial Personality Disorder

APD is characterized by lack of empathy or conscience, a difficulty controlling impulses and by manipulative behaviour.

Hyper-anxiety

Always fearful of something happening to them or their loved ones.

Controlling – manipulative

Need to be in charge. Believes that no one can do things better than they can.

Paranoid, passive, nervous, lacking confidence

Believes that everyone is out to get them. Lives their life in fear.

I want you to do an exercise now on different speech patterns of various types of people. To make it more interesting I am going to give some of them some of the more usual personalities we discussed earlier.

This is the scene: A group of people are standing at a city bus stop in a busy part of town.

In front of them, two cars collide and slide toward them, but are stopped by the gutter. The police are quickly on the scene.

I want you to write each person's reaction when they see it coming and what they would say when the cars collide. And then, what they would say about the accident when interviewed by the police as a witness. Have some fun with this. But try to work out what the speech pattern of each would be and how they would interpret the scene to the police.

These are the characters we have.

A lady about 30 with a baby in a pram. The woman is fussing with the baby and watching nervously for the bus. She suffers from *Hyper-anxiety*.

A well-dressed man carrying a briefcase. He is standing behind the mother, frowning at her and trying to keep his distance from the pram, but not lose his place in the queue. He is *controlling – manipulative*.

Two teenage girls with school bags bearing the crest of one of the more elite private schools, chatting and giggling. *Normal teens*

A couple of males, mid-twenties dressed in work clothes and covered in paint splotches, talking loudly and leering at the girls. *Normal guys.*

A twelve–year-old boy, scruffily dressed and without shoes, who asked everyone to lend him the fare for the bus. The mother gave it to him. He cowers behind the pram and keeps looking around as if he is afraid to be there. *Paranoid: A street kid, passive, nervous, lacking confidence.*

A couple of skin-head, tattooed guys, wearing vests and tight jeans, hanging at the back of the crowd and blatantly smoking weed. *Antisocial Personality Disorder.*

***

Now let's take that a bit further. I want you to write a short story using all of the elements we learned.

You have had a chance to develop your characters, so I want you to show who your characters are by their actions and dialogue.

Write a story of more than 100 words and up to 300 words, using the following guidelines:

The story will have lots of dialogue. So think of a situation that calls for that.

The dialogue should show:

* Their personality

* Their age

* Their education level

* A general idea of where they come from

* Their relationship to the character they are addressing.

* Their mood

You need to convey the setting and that setting should be in fitting with the mood of the characters.

Each character should have a distinctive voice, so we know who is speaking without tags.

Allow one of your characters to use slang or have a habitual way of speaking, but don't over-do it.

Vary the position of tags and action attributes.

Have fun with it but try to make it believable.

***

What else can you do to learn to write dialogue well?

The best way to learn is to see how the masters do it. Read within your genre and note techniques that really work.

Sit in front of the television and watch an episode of a favourite show, preferably in the genre you are writing. Listen to how the characters speak and respond.

At one point, the words the characters are speaking were just words on a page, written by a very well-paid writer. This may help tune your inner ear to the sound of dialogue.

While it's not a good idea to experiment with dialogue mechanics, it is fun to write dialogue in different ways to figure out which works best with your character. Go ahead and write a whole page in a foreign accent. Use slang in the next page, etc. Going overboard like this will open the mind to all sorts of possibilities. Writing good dialogue is a skill and talent that can be developed.

Numerous other devices exist to bring dialogue to life. Good writing requires curiosity, imagination, and inspiration. It also requires a knowledge of mechanics and craft.

As I said at the beginning, any writer who thinks writing dialogue is easy probably is not writing good dialogue.

If you have already written your story, go back and check for the things mentioned here. Read the dialogue out loud to see if it sounds natural and examine it to see if it fits the character.

The next writing guide will be on Editing. Once you have a first draft of your story, you then need to go back over it to check for things that could be improved and mistakes in grammar and punctuation. This guide will help you polish it until it shines.

CHARACTER QUESTIONAIRE:

This questionnaire is for all major characters in your story. But start with the main character. You can see that by answering these questions, you are building the personality of your characters. The first question you need to answer are these:

1. **What is your character's role in your story?**
2. **What physical attributes will they need for that role?**
3. **What emotional attributes will they need for that role?**
4. **What skills will they need for that role?**

The answers to those 4 questions will influence the answers to the following ones.

Now ask your characters these questions: This questionnaire should be filled in with the role the character has in your story in mind. Some question will only be relevant to certain genres and stories. You can add any other questions you think you need.

What is your name? How old are you? How tall? What is your build? What colour are your eyes, hair, skin?

Are you: Confident, Shy, Afraid, Weak, Strong, Clever, Dumb Average, Other?

Do you have a bad habit?

What are the things you like most about yourself?

What are the things you like least about yourself?

Describe how you think others see you?

Do you have any stand-out personal habits or way you dress?

Where were you raised? How would you describe your childhood?

What do/did your parents do for a living?

What were your parents like? Strict, Loving, Uncaring, Violent, other? What was/is your favourite class at school?

What are some experiences from your childhood that have affected the sort of person you are now?

Where do you now live? What is your job? Do you like it?

Are you rich, poor, or in-between?

Are you married/in a relationship? Is your relationship a happy one? If not, why?

Do you have any special belief systems?

What are your talents and skills? Do any of these talents or skills have a downside?

Do you have any mannerisms or speech quirks?

How many siblings do you have? What are your siblings' most annoying traits? What do you like about your siblings?

Who is your best friend? What are he/her best traits?

What do you look for in a friend? What do you look for in a partner?

If you had a secret, to whom would you tell it?

Of what are you afraid? What makes you happy?

What is your favourite food? What food makes you want to puke?

Who is your worst enemy? Why is he your enemy?

How do you feel about discipline?

Are you someone who fits in with society or someone who fights it?

How would you spend a typical day?

What do you want more than anything in the world?

www.ingramcontent.com/pod-product-compliance
Lightning Source LLC
Chambersburg PA
CBHW051949160426
43198CB00013B/2362